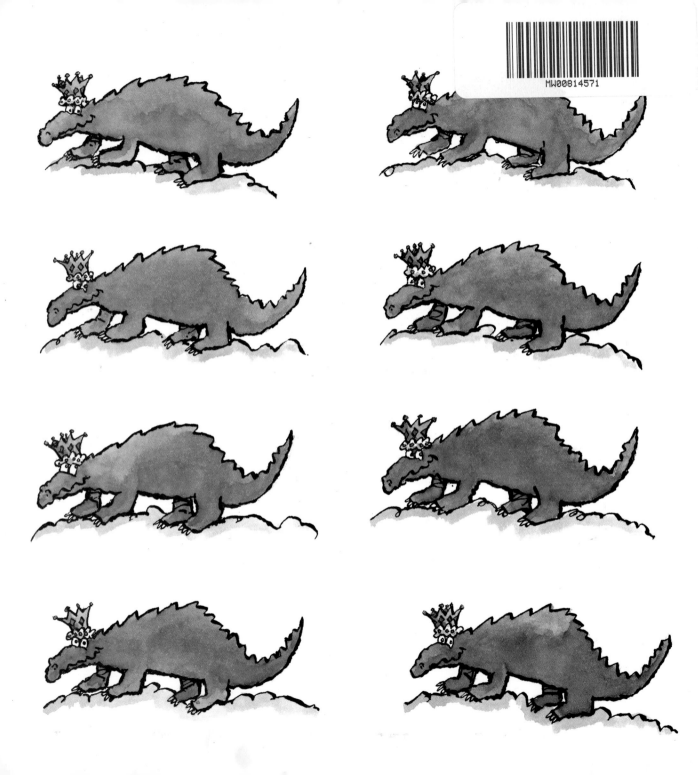

Oxford University Press, Walton Street, Oxford OX2 6DP

Oxford  New York  Toronto
Delhi  Bombay  Calcutta  Madras  Karachi
Petaling Jaya  Singapore  Hong Kong  Tokyo
Nairobi  Dar es Salaam  Cape Town
Melbourne  Auckland

and associated companies in
Beirut  Berlin  Ibadan  Nicosia

Oxford is a trade mark of Oxford University Press

Illustrations © Amelia Rosato 1987
Text © Donald Bisset 1987
First published 1987
ISBN 0 19 278216 9

British Library Cataloguing in Publication Data

Photoset by Tradespools Ltd, Frome, Somerset

Printed in Hong Kong

Donald Bisset

# OGG

Pictures by Amelia Rosato

Oxford University Press
Oxford · Toronto · Melbourne

Once upon a time there was a little baby bear named Chen Pu, who lived in a cave with his mother high up in the mountains of Tibet.

All day long the snow fell, but Chen Pu was warm and cosy in the cave. Sometimes, during the day, he went out to play, but at night he stayed at home close to his mother.

Whenever he looked out of the entrance to the cave he could see the stars shining and twinkling in the sky. And there was one star which shone brightest of all. It was a great big yellow star and it seemed to Chen Pu that it was *his* star.

All winter long Chen Pu lived in the cave with his mother. But when spring came she said to him, 'Chen Pu, you are a big bear now, you must go out into the world and have an adventure and then come back and see me and tell me about it.'

Chen Pu felt afraid, but his mother pushed him out of the cave with her nose. He wandered down the mountain till he came to a little frozen stream. And every day as he went downhill the weather grew warmer and the ice melted and the stream became a river. At night Chen Pu slept by its bank and looked up at his star, which seemed to stay with him wherever he went.

One night when Chen Pu was sitting sleepily by the river bank, looking up at his star, a big crocodile came along. He had lots and lots of sharp teeth. His name was Ogg and he was the King of the crocodiles. He was a bad crocodile and was always looking for things to steal.

When he saw Chen Pu looking up at the star he asked him, 'What are you staring at, little bear?'

'I'm looking at my star,' said Chen Pu. 'It is the most beautiful thing in the world.'

'Yes, it *is* beautiful,' said Ogg. 'It must be very valuable so I shall steal it and keep it for myself.'

'You mustn't steal it,' said Chen Pu. 'It's *my* star. I won't let you steal it.' But Ogg was very big and Chen Pu was only a small bear so what could he do?

Ogg called all the other animals who lived nearby and he told them to climb on his back one after the other. First an elephant stood on his back, then a rhinoceros climbed on the elephant's back, then a buffalo climbed on the rhinoceros's back, then a jackal climbed on the buffalo's back. Then a dog climbed up, then an otter, and a mongoose and a mole rat and, last of all, a little monkey climbed right to the top and reached out for the star. But he couldn't quite reach it.

He called out, 'I can't reach it!'

'Oh you are silly!' called Ogg. 'I'll get it myself.' He was just going to get out from underneath, but the other animals, who weren't stupid, shouted, 'Don't do that or we'll all fall down.'

'All right,' said Ogg, 'I'll think of another plan.'

The animals got down, and Ogg thought and thought, but he couldn't think what to do.

'Well, if I can't get the star I'll eat you up, little bear,' said Ogg.

'Oh, please don't do that,' said Chen Pu. 'I know how to help you.' Chen Pu, even though he was little, was very clever.

'All right, what is your plan?' said Ogg.

'Just wait a bit while I think!' said Chen Pu.

'Hurry up!' said Ogg. 'Or I'll eat you up.'

'Perhaps,' thought Chen Pu, 'if they all stood on Ogg's back again and I tickled him he'd wriggle and all the animals would fall down and squash him. No, that wouldn't do. I'm sure crocodiles aren't ticklish. Hm? I know!'

'Listen,' he said. 'All the animals standing on each other's backs here in the valley weren't high enough to reach the star. But if you all climbed a mountain you would be higher up and then you could reach it.'

'That's a good plan,' said Ogg. 'I won't eat you up, but I will steal your star.'

'Oho, we'll see!' thought Chen Pu.

He led Ogg and the other animals up the mountain, higher and higher. And the higher they went the colder it got and the animals started shivering. Still Chen Pu climbed on till they came to the part where the river was frozen. They went higher still and at last reached the top.

'Now I'll get the star,' said Ogg.
The animals all climbed on his back one after the other.
They were very cold and Ogg's teeth had started to chatter,
which was what Chen Pu had hoped would happen.

His teeth chattered and he shivered and made the animals wobble and, just as the little monkey was reaching out for the star, Ogg sneezed.

What a sneeze it was! It must have been the biggest sneeze in the world and all the animals came tumbling down, crash, right on Ogg's nose.

'Oooooooh, ouch!' said Ogg. 'My poor teeth!' Ogg had about fifty teeth and every one of them ached. Ogg sneezed again. It was a bigger sneeze than ever and made him start to slip downhill on the ice.

'Atishoo!' he sneezed an even bigger sneeze and slid down that mountain like a rocket, sneezing all the way.

The animals watched as he got smaller and smaller in the distance till he disappeared. And that was the last Chen Pu ever saw of him.

Later that night, when the animals had gone home, Chen Pu sat and looked up at his star. How it twinkled in the frosty air. Then he slept for a bit and, next day, went home to his mother.

'Have you had a nice adventure, Chen Pu?' she asked.

'Yes,' said Chen Pu and told her all about it.

His mother licked him with her soft tongue, then curled round him so that he was nice and warm. Then she went to sleep. But Chen Pu lay looking up at his star. Presently he fell asleep.

After a while the snow began to fall quietly and gently all round him till all the world was white. Up above in the night sky there shone, clear and bright, a lovely shining yellow star. Chen Pu's star.

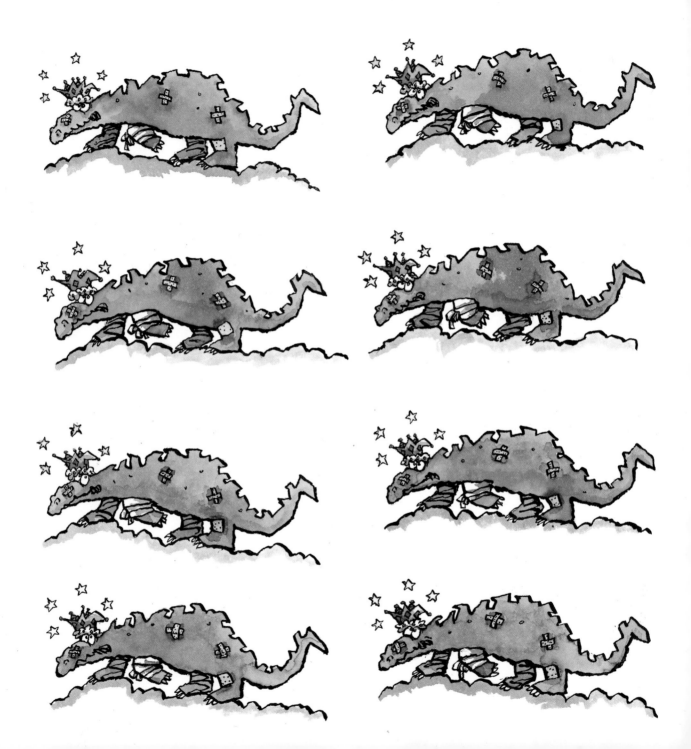